0 TO Bitch IN 10 SECONDS OR LESS

Quips and Comebacks
for Quick-Witted Women

0 TO Bitch IN 10 SECONDS OR LESS

Quips and Comebacks
for Quick-Witted Women

Amy Hatch

SOURCEBOOKS HYSTERIA™
AN IMPRINT OF SOURCEBOOKS, INC.®
NAPERVILLE, ILLINOIS

Bitch

IN 10 SECONDS OR LESS

Quips and Comebacks for Quick-Witted Women

Published by Sourcebooks Hysteria, an imprint of Sourcebooks, Inc.
P.O. Box 4410, Naperville, Illinois 60567-4410
(630) 961-3900
FAX: (630) 961-2168
www.sourcebooks.com

ISBN 1-4022-0382-9

Printed and bound in Canada

WC 10 9 8 7 6 5

To Catherine, Macenzie, Heidi, Ashley, and my sisters—for all the love, laughter, advice, and support you have given me.

L★ve and Sex

**Food is like sex:
when you abstain,
even the worst stuff
begins to look good.**

—*Beth McCollister*

Love is a game that two can play
and both can win.

—*Eva Gabor*

If he says that you're too good for him,
believe it!

—*Debbie Farson*

Women might be able to fake orgasms,
but men can fake whole relationships.

—*Sharon Stone*

You marry out of your greatest love,
or your greatest fear.

—Taxi Driver's Wisdom, *Joanne Dugan and Risa Mickenberg*

Clinton lied.
A man might forget
where he parks
or where he lives,
but he never forgets
oral sex,
no matter how bad it is.

—Former First Lady Barbara Bush

Men marry women
with the hope they
will never change.
Women marry men
with the hope they
will change.
Invariably they
are both disappointed.

—*Albert Einstein*

If you chase it, it will run.

—*Variously Ascribed*

A dress makes no sense
unless it inspires men
to want to take it off you.

—*Francoise Sagan*

Honesty is the key to a relationship.
If you can fake that, you're in.

—*Richard Jeni*

Give a man a free hand
and he'll run it all over you.

—*Mae West*

If you never wanted
to kill your mate,
you've never
been in love.

—*Chris Rock*

There are
easier things in life than
finding a good man—
nailing Jell-O to a tree,
for instance.

—*Unknown*

I have found you need someone to love
while you are looking for
someone to love.

—*Shelagh Delaney*

Opposites attract—
and then aggravate.

—*Joy Browne*

Forget about the Rules for Catching
a Husband. What about Rules for
Catching a Life?

—*Susan Jane Gilman*

The Bible contains six admonishments to
homosexuals and three hundred and
sixty-two admonishments to heterosexuals.
This doesn't mean that God doesn't
love heterosexuals. It just means
they need more supervision.

—*Lynn Larner*

Right now there are two things in my life that need to be done: me and my laundry. I want to marry a man who can do both.

—*Ophira Edut*

13

Lead me not into temptation; I can find the way myself.

—*Rita Mae Brown*

Immature love says, "I love you
because I need you." Mature love says,
"I need you because I love you."

—*Erich Fromm*

Men are like parking spaces...
the good ones are either too small
or they are already taken.

—*Shirley Eujeste*

Not every meaningful relationship
has to last forever to be meaningful.

—*Unknown*

I am not addicted to being miserable;
I am just addicted to miserable people.

—*Delilah*

**A woman
has the last word
in any argument.
Anything a man
says after that
is the beginning of
a new argument.**

—Unknown

If you don't like someone,
the way he holds his spoon
will make you furious;
if you do like him,
he can turn his
plate over in your lap
and you won't mind.

—*Irving Becker*

Don't put an absurdly high value on your guy. Think of the millions of other girls doing without him, yet able to bear it.

—*Orfea Sybil*

The only thing harder than being alone is being with the wrong person.

—*Unknown*

Love at first sight is
certainly a most amusing thing,
especially to the bystanders.

—Eliza Leslie

The only time a woman really succeeds
in changing a man is when he is a baby.

—Natalie Wood

God gave women
intuition and femininity.
Used properly,
the combination easily
jumbles the brain of
any man I've ever met.

—*Farrah Fawcett*

Shopping
is better than sex.
If you're not satisfied
after shopping you can make
an exchange for something
you really like.

—Adrienne Gusoff

Time wounds all heels.

—*Unknown*

I don't believe in divorce.
I believe in widowhood.

—*Carolyn Green*

No woman can
take a man away from you
unless he's willing to leave.

—*Unknown*

The trouble with relationships...
people change
and forget to tell each other.

—*Lillian Hellman*

I didn't realize
until quite late in life
that women were
supposed to be
the inferior sex.

—*Katharine Hepburn*

You see a lot of smart guys with dumb women, but you hardly ever see a smart woman with a dumb guy.

—Erica Jong

I've had an exciting life.
I married for love and
got a little money along with it.

—*Rose Fitzgerald Kennedy*

A man on a date wonders
if he'll get lucky.
The woman already knows.

—*Monica Piper*

I rely on my personality
for birth control.

—*Liz Winston*

When women go wrong,
men go right after them.

—*Mae West*

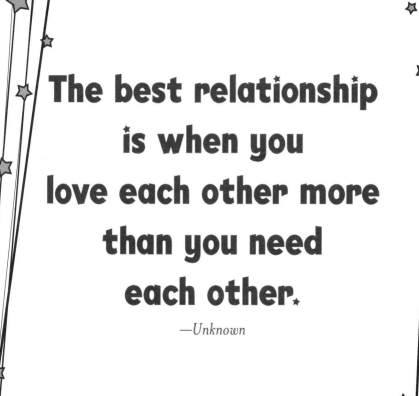

The best relationship is when you love each other more than you need each other.

—*Unknown*

I have not yet
been able to answer
the great question that
has never been answered:
What does a woman want?

—*Sigmund Freud*

I think—
therefore I'm single.

—*Lizz Winstead*

According to a new survey,
women say they feel more comfortable
undressing in front of men than they do
undressing in front of other women.
They say that women are too judgmental,
where, of course, men are just grateful.

—*Robert De Niro*

If women didn't exist,
all the money in the world
would have no meaning.

—*Aristotle Onassis*

A woman of thirty-five thinks
of having children.
A man of thirty-five thinks
of dating children.

—*Murphy's Laws of Sex*

Friend: A member of the opposite sex in your acquaintance who has some flaw which makes sleeping with him/her totally unappealing.

—Dictionary of Dating

When I want to end
a relationship I just say,
"You know, I love you.
I want to marry you. I want
to have your children."
Sometimes
they leave skid marks.

—*Rita Rudner*

If you love something, set it free.
If it doesn't come back,
hunt it down and kill it.

—Unknown

Relationships give us a reason to live.
Revenge.

—Ronny Shakes

Love men, but keep your girlfriends;
only a girlfriend understands why it is,
suddenly, after years of shopping
together, you don't have a thing to wear
for a date on Friday night.

—*"Dear Prudence"*

Can you imagine a world without men?
No crime and lots of happy, fat women.

—*Marion Smith*

Girlfriends
don't let girlfriends
drink and
take ugly men home.

—Unknown

If God wanted women to bend over he'd put diamonds on the floor.

—*Joan Rivers*

Love is the answer,
but while you're waiting for the answer
sex raises some pretty good questions.

—*Woody Allen,* Woody Allen: Clown Prince of American Humor

Sex—
the thing that takes up the least
amount of time and causes
the most amount of trouble.

—*John Barrymore*

A kiss can be a comma, a question
mark, or an exclamation point.
That's basic spelling that
every woman ought to know.

—*Mistinguette*

Sex is a lot like air;
it doesn't seem important
unless you aren't getting any of it.

—*Unknown*

When
you've got them
by the balls,
their hearts and minds
will follow.

—Colson's Law

Pizza is a lot like sex.
When it's good,
it's really good.
When it's bad,
it's still pretty good.

—*Unknown*

Is sex dirty?
Only if it's done right.

—*Woody Allen,* Everything You Always Wanted to Know about Sex

Being a woman
is terribly difficult trade,
since it consists principally
in dealing with men.

—*Joseph Conrad*

If love is the answer,
could you please rephrase the question?

—Lily Tomlin

The perfect lover is one
who turns into a pizza at 4 a.m.

—*Charles Pierce*

The one
who loves the least
controls the relationship.

—Robert Newton Anthony

The appropriate age
for marriage
is around eighteen for girls
and thirty-seven for men.

—*Aristotle*

Sometimes I wonder if men and women really suit each other. Perhaps they should live next door to each other and just visit now and then.

—*Katharine Hepburn*

A girl can wait for the right man to come along, but in the meantime that still doesn't mean she can't have a wonderful time with all the wrong ones.

—*Cher*

Love is a matter of chemistry;
sex is a matter of physics.

—*Unknown*

If it is your time,
love will track you down
like a cruise missile.

—*Lynda Barry*

It is better
to be unfaithful than
to be faithful
without wanting to be.

—*Brigitte Bardot*

No matter how
lovesick a woman is,
she shouldn't take
the first pill
that comes along.

—Joyce Brothers

If you want to say it with flowers,
a single rose says: "I'm cheap!"

—*Delta Burke*

Women's Rule of Thumb:
If it has tires or testicles,
you're going to have trouble with it.

—*Unknown*

Anybody who believes that the way
to a man's heart is through his stomach
flunked geography.

—*Robert Byrne*

The old theory was "Marry an older
man, because they're more mature."
But the new theory is "Men don't
mature. Marry a younger one."

—*Rita Rudner*

**No one
will ever win the
battle of the sexes;
there is
too much fraternizing
with the enemy.**

—*Henry Kissinger*

53

Marrying a man is like buying something you've been admiring for a long time in a shop window. You may love it when you get it home, but it doesn't always go with everything else in the house.

—Jean Kerr

The trouble with some women
is they get all excited about nothing—
and then they marry him.

—*Cher*

No one worth possessing
can be quite possessed.

—*Sara Teasdale*

Men and women, women and men...
It will never work.

—*Erica Jong*

In America sex is an obsession;
in other parts of the world
it is just a fact.

—*Marlene Dietrich*

A man can sleep around,
no questions asked,
but if a woman makes
nineteen or twenty
mistakes she's a tramp.

—*Joan Rivers*

No woman
ever hates a man
for being in love with her,
but many a woman
hates a man
for being a friend to her.

—*Alexander Pope*

Love may be blind, but it certainly
finds its way around the dark.

—*Unknown*

Most girls are attracted
to the simple things in life—
like men.

—*Henny Youngman*

A kiss
is a lovely trick designed to stop speech
when words become unnecessary.

—*Ingrid Bergman*

Women with a past interest men...
they hope history will repeat itself.

—*Mae West*

Girls are so [odd]
you never know
what they mean. They say
No when they mean Yes,
and drive a man out of his
wits for the fun of it.

—*Louisa May Alcott*

In passing, also,
I would like to say
that the first time
Adam had the chance
he laid the blame
on a woman.

—*Nancy Astor*

Don't marry for money;
you can borrow it cheaper.

—*Scottish Proverb*

Sex is not love. Love is chocolate.
And puppies. And TiVo.

—*Aisha Tyler*

Most women set out to change a man
and find that when they have
changed him they do not want him.

—*Marlene Dietrich*

I hate women because
they always know where things are.

—*James Thurber*

It was a woman who drove me to drink, and I never had the courtesy to thank her for it.

—W. C. Fields

A liberated woman
is one who has sex
before marriage
and a job after.

—*Gloria Steinem*

Love will find a lay.

—*Robert Byrne*

Husbands are like fires;
they go out if unattended.

—*Zsa Zsa Gabor*

I'm as pure as the driven slush.

—*Tallulah Bankhead*

Anyone who eats three meals a day
should understand why cookbooks
outsell sex books three to one.

—*L. M. Boyd*

A wife lasts
only for the length
of the marriage,
but an ex-wife is there
for the rest of your life.

—*Jim Samuels*

Eighty percent of
married men cheat
in America.
The rest cheat in Europe.

—*Jackie Mason*

Anyone who says he can
see through women is missing a lot.

—*Groucho Marx*

The happiest liaisons are based
on mutual misunderstanding.

—*La Rochefoucauld*

Love is what happens to men
and women who don't know each other.

—*W. Somerset Maugham*

A terrible thing
happened again last night—nothing.

—*Phyllis Diller*

Kissing is a means of getting two people so close together that they can't see anything wrong with each other.

—Rene Yasenek

Enjoy yourself.
If you can't
enjoy yourself,
enjoy somebody else.

—*Jack Schaefer*

He was like the flesh and blood
equivalent of a DKNY dress—you know
it's not your style, but it's right there
so you try it on anyway.

—*Sarah Jessica Parker* as *Carrie Bradshaw* on Sex in the City

I was nauseous and tingly all over. I was
either in love or I had smallpox.

—*Woody Allen*

The Facts of Life

It's always something.

—*Gilda Radner*

You know you have found happiness
when you stop looking for it.

—*Unknown*

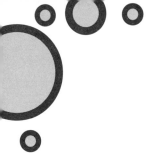

Having something to say is overrated.

—*Lara Adair*

The problem with people
who have no vices is that,
generally,
you can be pretty sure
they're going to have some
pretty annoying virtues.

—*Elizabeth Taylor*

No pressure, no diamonds.

—Mary Case

Life is sexually transmitted
and terminal.

—Unknown

Your character is who you are
when the lights are out.

—*Julie Bowen*

In three words I can sum up
everything I know about life:
it goes on.

—*Robert Frost*

I believe in
getting into hot water;
it keeps you clean.

—*G. K. Chesterton*

"Normal" is getting dressed
in clothes that you buy for work
and driving through traffic in a car
that you are still paying for—
in order to get to the job you need to
pay for the clothes and the car and
the house you leave vacant all day
so you can afford to live in it.

—Ellen DeGeneres

You always glide
just before you hit bottom.

—*Unknown*

Most conversations
are simply monologues delivered
in the presence of witnesses.

—*Margaret Millar*

An apology is a good way
to have the last word.

—Unknown

I hate to spread rumors,
but what else can you do with them?

—Amanda Lear

Gossip is what you say about the objects of flattery when they aren't present.

—P. J. O'Rourke

Whoever said money can't buy happiness didn't know where to shop.

—*Unknown*

It is easier to get forgiveness
than to get permission.

—*Unknown*

Instant gratification
is not soon enough.

—*Meryl Streep*

I have enough money
to last me the rest of my life,
unless I buy something.

—*Jackie Mason*

Money is always there,
but the pockets change.

—*Gertrude Stein*

Some days
you're the dog,
and some days
you're the hydrant.

—Unknown

You are not drunk
if you can lie on the floor
without holding on.

—*Joe E. Lewis*

Humor is truth, only faster.

—*Gilda Radner*

Alcohol may not be the answer,
but it helps you forget the question.

—*Henry Mon*

The only thing that has to be finished
by next Tuesday is next Monday.

—*Jennifer Unlimited*

It is only possible to live happily ever
after on a day-to-day basis.

—*Margaret Bonnano*

Nothing is so simple
that it can't
be screwed up.

—Unknown

Opportunity may
knock only once,
but temptation
leans on the doorbell.

—*Unknown*

Show me a good loser
and I'll show you a loser.

—*Paul Newman*

Reality is that which, when you stop
believing in it, doesn't go away.

—*Phillip K. Dick*

It is a common delusion that
you can make things better by
talking about them.

—*Dame Rose Macauley*

I do not want people to be agreeable,
as it saves me the trouble of liking them.

—*Jane Austen*

The statistics on sanity are that one out of every four Americans is suffering from some form of mental illness. Think of your three best friends. If they're okay, then it's you.

—*Rita Mae Brown*

The problem is not that there are problems. The problem is expecting otherwise and thinking that having problems is a problem.

—*Theodore Rubin*

Reality is the leading cause of stress
amongst those in touch with it.

—*Jane Wagner*

When everything's coming your way,
you're in the wrong lane.

—*Unknown*

Everything happens
to everyone sooner or later—
if there is time enough.

—*George Bernard Shaw*

Advice is what we ask for
when we already know the answer
but wish we didn't.

—*Erica Jong*

Rules
are for people
who don't know how
to get around them.

—*Tori Harrison*

At the end of the night,
or the end of the party,
when everyone goes home,
remember
you're stuck with yourself.

—*Layne Staley*

Only a few things are really important.

—*Marie Dressler*

Normal is in the eye of the beholder.

—*Whoopi Goldberg*

I'm not funny.
What I am is brave.
—*Lucille Ball*

If you want to make God laugh,
tell him your plans.
—*Variously Ascribed*

Laugh and the world laughs with you. Cry and you cry with your girlfriends.

—*Laurie Kuslansky*

I have found
that the only things
I have to regret
are the things I did not do.

—*Sharon Osbourne*

Maybe all one can do
is hope to end up with the right regrets.

—*Arthur Miller*

The pure and simple truth is rarely pure
and never simple.

—*Oscar Wilde*

If you always do what you've always done,
you'll always get
what you've always gotten.

—*Unknown*

When you're drinking martinis
and your martini glass is full of tears,
you gotta ask yourself, is the Universe
trying to tell me something?

—*Plum Sykes,* Bergdorf Blondes

The greatest pleasure in life is doing what people say you cannot do.

—*Walter Bagehot*

When we ask for advice, we are usually looking for an accomplice.

—*Marquis de la Grange*

Life is full of misery, loneliness, and
suffering, and it is over much too soon.

—*Woody Allen*

If you can't be a good example,
then you'll just have to be
a horrible warning.

—*Catherine Aird*

Every time I close the door on reality
it comes in through the windows.

—*Jennifer Unlimited*

The most welcome person is the one
who knows when to go.

—*Unknown*

If a man
smiles all the time
he's probably
selling something
that doesn't work.

—*George Carlin*

Those of you
who think you
know everything
are annoying
to those of us who do.

—*Ricky Gervais*

Work is a dull way to get rich.

—*Neal Ascherson*

A gossip is someone who talks to you
about others, a bore is someone who
talks to you about himself, and
a brilliant conversationalist is someone
who talks to you about yourself.

—*Lisa Kirk*

A lottery ticket is to remind us
that we're equals underneath it all.

—*Unknown*

Nothing is as good as it seems
beforehand.

—*George Eliot*

Life's
under no obligation
to give us
what we expect.

—*Margaret Mitchell*

When you are unhappy,
is there anything
more maddening than to be
told you should be content
with what you've got?

—*Kathleen Norris*

Jealousy—
all the fun you think they are having.

—*Unknown*

Politeness is half good manners
and half good lying.

—*Mary Wilson Little*

Never think you've seen the last
of anything.

—*Eudora Welty*

After all, what is reality anyway?
Nothing but a collective hunch.

—*Lily Tomlin*

Have you ever noticed? Anybody going slower than you is an idiot, and anyone going faster than you is a maniac.

—*George Carlin*

A true friend is someone who is there for you when he'd rather be somewhere else.

—Len Wein

The other line *does* move faster.

—Etorre's Observation

There is no pleasure
in having nothing to do; the fun is
in having lots to do and not doing it.

—Mary Wilson Little

Things are going to get a lot worse
before they get worse.

—*Lily Tomlin*

People who claim they don't let little
things bother them have never slept
in a room with a single mosquito.

—*Unknown*

How long a minute is depends on which side of the bathroom door you're on.

—*Unknown*

If it jams—
force it.
If it breaks,
it needed replacing anyway.

—*Lowery's Law*

Everybody goes different ways
to see the same thing.

—*Risa Mickenberg*

If it happens,
it must be possible.

—*Murphy's Laws*

Too much of a good thing
can be wonderful.

—*Mae West*

Conquest is easy. Control is not.

—*William Shatner as Captain James T. Kirk in* Star Trek

Good judgment is
the result of experience.
Experience is the result
of bad judgment.

—*Fred Brooks*

Don't believe your friends
when they ask you
to be honest with them.
All they really want is
to be maintained in
the good opinion they have
of themselves.

—*Eustace Budgell*

You can't be truly rude
until you understand good manners.

—*Rita Mae Brown*

Beer is proof that God loves us
and wants us to be happy.

—*Benjamin Franklin*

Happiness is good health
and a bad memory.

—*Ingrid Bergman*

People who drink light beer
don't like the taste of beer;
they just like to pee a lot.

—*Advertisement, Capital Brewery*

An alcoholic is anyone you don't like who drinks slightly more than you do.

—*Dylan Thomas*

The cocktail party is a device for paying off obligations to people that you don't want to invite to dinner.

—*Charles Smith*

Cocaine is God's way of saying,
"you're making too much money."

—*Robin Williams*

If things appear to be going well,
you may have overlooked something.

—*Unknown*

Misery no longer loves company.
Nowadays it insists on it.

—*Russell Wayne Baker*

Good girls go to heaven;
bad girls go everywhere.

—*Helen Gurley Brown*

The quickest way
to know a woman
is to go
shopping with her.

—Marcelene Cox

The true measure of
a man is how he
treats someone who can
do him absolutely no good.

—*Samuel Johnson*

The nice thing about being a celebrity
is that if you bore people,
they think it's their fault.

—*Henry Kissinger*

If everything seems under control,
you're just not going fast enough.

—*Mario Andretti*

Few things are harder to put up with than a good example.

—*Mark Twain*

The mistakes
are all waiting to be made.

—*Savielly Grigorievitch Tartakower*

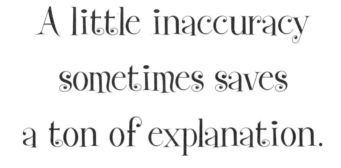

A little inaccuracy
sometimes saves
a ton of explanation.

—*H. H. Munro*

Three o'clock is always
too late or
too early for
anything you want to do.

—*Jean-Paul Sartre*

If no one uses it,
there's a reason.

—*Unknown*

He who hesitates is a damned fool.

—*Mae West*

Friends may come and go,
but enemies accumulate.

—*Thomas Jones*

Hell is paved with good Samaritans.

—*William M. Holden*

The difference between fiction and reality? Fiction has to make sense.

—*Tom Clancy*

Everything is funny as long as it is happening to somebody else.

—*Will Rogers*

Constantly talking
isn't necessarily communicating.

—*Jim Carrey as Joel Barish*
in Eternal Sunshine of the Spotless Mind

True friends
stab you in the front.

—*Oscar Wilde*

Ultimately, magic finds you,
if you let it.

—*Tony Wheeler*

The trouble with being punctual
is that nobody's there to appreciate it.

—*Franklin P. Jones*

I'll not listen to reason.
Reason always means
what someone else has
got to say.

—Elizabeth Gaskell

It is dangerous
to be sincere unless
you are also stupid.

—*George Bernard Shaw*

Trust in God,
but always remember to lock the car.

—*Unknown*

If you haven't got anything nice to say
about anybody, come sit next to me.

—*Alice Roosevelt Longworth*

He who laughs last,
didn't get it.

—*Helen Giangregorio*

When women are depressed
they either eat or go shopping.
Men invade another country.

—*Elayne Boosler*

I personally think that
we developed language
because of
our deep inner need
to complain.

—Jane Wagner

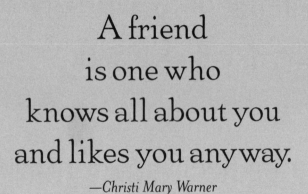

A friend
is one who
knows all about you
and likes you anyway.

—*Christi Mary Warner*

Bigger doesn't necessarily mean better.
Sunflowers aren't better than violets.

—*Edna Ferber*

Sanity is a cozy lie.

—*Susan Sontag*

It's useless to hold a person to anything
they say while they are in love, drunk,
or running for office.

—*Shirley MacLaine*

Reality is something you rise above.

—*Liza Minnelli*

You take your life in your own hands, and what happens? A terrible thing— no one to blame.

—*Erica Jong*

You can fool
all of the people
some of the time,
and some of the people
all of the time.
And that's sufficient.

—*Rose King*

Well-behaved women rarely
make history.

—*Laurel Thatcher Ulrich*

The adventure is worthwhile in itself.

—*Amelia Earhart*

Mistakes are part of the dues one pays
for a full life.

—*Sophia Loren*

The way I see it,
if you want the rainbow,
you gotta put up with the rain.

—*Dolly Parton*

You grow up
the day you have your
first real laugh
at yourself.

—*Ethel Barrymore*

Conscience
is the inner voice
that warns us
that someone
may be looking.

—*H. L. Mencken*

To err is human,
but it feels divine.

—*Mae West*

Unexpected things happen more often
than those you hope for.

—*Unknown*

You're never too old to grow up.

—*Shirley Conran*

The fact that you could die tomorrow frees you up to appreciate your life now.

—*Angelina Jolie*

Not only
is life a bitch,
it has puppies.

—*Adrienne Gustoff*

One of the advantages
of being disorderly is
that one is constantly
making exciting discoveries.

—*A. A. Milne*

Home is where you go when you're tired
of being polite to people.

—*Unknown*

Intuition: That strange instinct that
tells a woman she is right,
whether she is or not.

—*Unknown*

Life is something to do
when you can't get to sleep.

—*Fran Lebowitz*

The truth will set you free.
But first, it will piss you off.

—*Gloria Steinem*

When a man gives his opinion, he's a man. When a woman gives her opinion, she's a bitch.

—*Bette Davis*

The trouble
with talking nicely is that,
unfortunately,
some people don't hear you
until you scream.

—*Stefanie Powers*

Hope is the feeling you have that
the feeling you have isn't permanent.

—*Jean Kerr*

Show me a woman who doesn't feel
guilty and I'll show you a man.

—*Erica Jong*

We're all in this alone.

—*Lily Tomlin*

Expecting life to treat you well
because you are a good person
is like expecting a bull not to charge you
because you are a vegetarian.

—*Shari Barr*

Guilt is often
the price we pay willingly
for what we are
going to do anyway.

—Isabelle Holland

I have yet
to see any problem,
however complicated,
which, when looked at
in the right way,
did not become
still more complicated.

—Poul Anderson

Nothing that costs only a dollar
is worth having.

—*Elizabeth Arden*

Being a woman is of special interest
only to aspiring male transsexuals.
To actual women it is simply a good
excuse not to play football.

—*Fran Lebowitz*

It is amazing how nice people are to you
when they know you are going away.

—*Michael Arlen*

I drink to make other people
more interesting.

—*George Jean Nathan*

I've always been
interested in people,
but I've never liked them.

—*Somerset Maugham*

Life is hard.
After all,
it kills you.

—*Katharine Hepburn*

I never know how much of
what I say is true.

—*Bette Midler*

Reality is a crutch for people
who can't cope with drugs.

—*Lily Tomlin*

The Beauty Within

Women dress alike all over the world:
they dress to annoy other women.

—*Elsa Schiaparelli*

There is nothing sexier
than confidence.

—*Unknown*

Even I don't look like
Cindy Crawford
when I wake up
in the morning.

—*Cindy Crawford*

The chief excitement
in a woman's life
is spotting women who are
fatter than she is.

—*Helen Rowland*

Say what you want about long dresses,
but they cover a multitude of sins.

—*Mae West*

I never go out unless I look like Joan
Crawford the movie star. If you want
to see the girl next door, go next door.

—*Joan Crawford*

If you don't show up at a party,
people will assume it's because
you've gained weight.

—*Stephanie Vanderkellen*

The woman who puts the right number
of candles on her birthday cake
is playing with fire.

—*Unknown*

**Sex appeal
is 50 percent
what you've got
and 50 percent
what people think
you've got.**

—*Sophia Loren*

Smile.
It's the second
best thing you can do
with your lips.

—*Unknown*

We are so vain that we even care for
the opinions of those we don't care for.

—*Marie Ebner von Eschenbach*

If you look good and dress well,
you don't need a purpose in life.

—*Robert Pante*

Being perfectly well-dressed
gives a feeling of tranquility
that religion is powerless to bestow.

—*Ralph Waldo Emerson*

Any piece of clothing can be sexy with
a passionate woman inside it.

—*Unknown*

The second day
of a diet is always
easier than the first.
By the second day,
you're off it.

—*Jackie Gleason*

I like having
a good pair of tits
and a good ass.
If I didn't,
I don't think
I'd feel attractive.

—*Kate Winslet*

If the shoe fits,
it's too expensive.

—*Adrienne Gusoff*

Where there is willpower,
there is less weight to gain.

—*Dieter's Proverb*

I base most of my fashion taste
on what doesn't itch.

—*Gilda Radner*

Beauty, to me, is about being
comfortable in your own skin;
that, or a kick-ass red lipstick.

—*Gwyneth Paltrow*

Your body is a temple;
a nice, clean, hot,
curvy temple.

—Aisha Tyler

Don't spend your life
as a pretty bitch...
God will send you back
nice and ugly!

—*Fritz*

Jewelry takes people's minds
off your wrinkles.

—*Sonja Henie*

Thirty-five is when you finally
get your head together and
your body starts falling apart.

—*Caryn Leschen*

You start out happy that
you have no hips or boobs.
All of a sudden you get them,
and it feels sloppy. Then just when
you start liking them, they start sagging.

—*Cindy Crawford*

You're only as good as your last haircut.

—*Fran Lebowitz*

**It is better
to be beautiful
than to be good.
But...it is better
to be good
than to be ugly.**

—*Oscar Wilde*

Don't cry for a man who's left you. The next one may fall for your smile.

—Mae West

A lady is one who never
shows her underwear unintentionally.

—*Lillian Day*

A narcissist is someone
better looking than you are.

—*Gore Vidal*

I have a great diet. You're allowed to eat anything you want, but you must eat it with naked fat people.

—*Ed Bluestone*

I'm not into working out.
My philosophy: No pain, no pain.

—*Carol Leifer*

Any girl
can be glamorous.
All you have to do
is stand still
and look stupid.

—*Hedy Lamarr*

The problem with beauty
is that it's like being
born rich
and getting poorer.

—*Joan Collins*

Beauty is in the eye of
the beer holder.

—*Unknown*

If you look like your passport photo,
you're too ill to travel.

—*Will Kommen*

If you're not beguiling by age twelve,
forget it.

—*Lucy of* Peanuts *(Charles Schulz)*

Beauty fades. Dumb is forever.

—*Unknown*

The average girl would rather have beauty than brains because she knows the average man can see much better than he can think.

—*Anonymous*

Secrets

of

Success

and the Lack Thereof

Never miss a good chance to shut up.

—*Will Rogers*

If you must step on someone to get ahead, use a very sharp heel!

—*Unknown*

All the best deals are made by those that can afford to say no.

—Ivan Hoffman

We must believe in luck. For how else can we explain the success of those we do not like?

—Jean Cocteau

The thing women have yet to learn
is nobody gives you the power.
You just take it.

—*Roseanne Barr*

A successful man is one who makes
more money than his wife can spend.
A successful woman
is one who can find such a man.

—*Lana Turner*

Never look as if you are lost.
Always look as if you know exactly where
you are going. If you don't know where
you are going, head straight for the bar.

—*Joan Collins*

Usefulness is not impaired
by imperfection. You can drink
from a chipped cup.

—*Greta K. Nagel*

Obstacles are
those frightful things
you see when
you take your eyes
off the goal.

—*Variously Ascribed*

A failure
is someone who
saw the possibilities
and chose not
to experience them.

—*Unknown*

You can have anything you want in life
if you dress for it.

—*Edith Head*

People who drink to drown
their sorrows should be told that sorrow
knows how to swim.

—*Ann Landers*

Seize the moment. Remember all those women on the *Titanic* who waved off the dessert cart.

—*Erma Bombeck*

Failure is God's way of saying, "Excuse me, but you're moving in the wrong direction."

—*Oprah Winfrey*

I have failed
over and over again
in my life.
And that is why
I succeed.

—*Michael Jordan*

You shouldn't step on people
to get ahead,
but you can step over them
if they are in the way.

—*Star Jones*

Whenever I am caught between two evils, I take the one I have never tried.

—*Mae West*

Don't hate yourself in the morning— sleep till noon.

—*Unknown*

Never do anything for yourself
that others can do for you.

—*Agatha Christie*

Even if we don't want it,
we can benefit from it.

—*Unknown*

You can cry, but don't let it stop you. Don't cry in one spot— cry as you continue to move.

—*Kina*

Don't compromise yourself. You are all you've got.

—*Janis Joplin*

Do what you are afraid to do.

—*Mary Emerson*

If you are going to be able to look back
on something and laugh about it,
you may as well laugh about it now.

—*Marie Osmond*

I've been rich and I've been poor.
Rich is better.

—*Sophie Tucker*

Never bite off less than you can chew.

—*Unknown*

People tell me
I've been lucky,
but I've worked very hard
to be lucky.

—*Molly Sims*

A good rule of thumb
is if you've made it to
thirty-five and your job still
requires that you wear
a nametag, you've made
a vocational error.

—Dennis Miller

The secret of having a personal life
is not answering too many
questions about it.

—*Joan Collins*

Nobody can make you feel inferior
without your permission.

—*Eleanor Roosevelt*

If you worried about falling off the bike,
you'd never get on.

—*Lance Armstrong*

To avoid criticism,
do nothing, say nothing, be nothing.

—*Elbert Hubbard*

Remember that not getting what you want is sometimes a wonderful stroke of luck.

—*Unknown*

Anything's possible
if you've got
enough nerve.

—*J. K. Rowling*

The beaten track
does not lead to new pastures.

—*Indira Gandhi*

Great love and great achievements
involve great risk.

—*Unknown*

Remember that a kick in the ass
is still a step forward.

—*Variously Ascribed*

Even if you're on the right track,
you'll get run over if you just sit there.

—*Will Rogers*

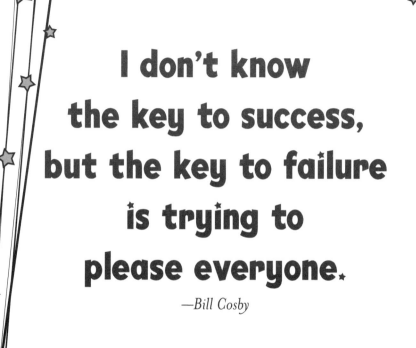

I don't know
the key to success,
but the key to failure
is trying to
please everyone.

—*Bill Cosby*

237

Dress for the job you want, not the job you have.

—*Kevin Dunn as Mr. Mercer in* Picture Perfect

When you lose, don't lose the lesson.

—*Unknown*

It's not how fast you get there,
but how long you stay.

—*Patty Berg*

Happy is harder than money.
Anybody who thinks money will make
you happy hasn't got money.

—*David Geffen*

Whether you think that you can
or that you can't, you are usually right.

—*Henry Ford*

Surviving is important. Thriving is elegant.

—*Maya Angelou*

When opportunity knocks,
open the damn door!

—Unknown

If at first you don't succeed, try again.
Then quit. There's no use
in being a damn fool about it.

—*W. C. Fields*

If you can't convince 'em, confuse 'em.

—*Unknown*

The people who say
"I told you so" are winning.

—*Laron Reynolds*

Never interrupt your enemy when
he is making a mistake.

—*Napoleon Bonaparte*

There are only
two tragedies in life:
one is not getting
what one wants, and
the other is getting it.

—Oscar Wilde

Don't take
yourself too seriously.
And don't be too serious
about not taking yourself
too seriously.

—*Howard Ogden*

If you are going through hell,
keep going.

—*Sir Winston Churchill*

He who dies with the most toys is,
nonetheless, still dead.

—*Unknown*

The secret of success is to know
something nobody else knows.

—*Aristotle Onassis*

It's kind of fun to do the impossible.

—*Walt Disney*

Life consists not in holding good cards, but in playing those you hold well.

—*Josh Billings*

Love your enemies— they'll hate it!

—*Unknown*

A positive attitude may not solve all your problems, but it will annoy enough people to make it worth the effort.

—*Herm Albright*

Accept good advice gracefully—
as long as it doesn't interfere with what
you intended to do in the first place.

—*Gene Brown*

Be nice to people on your way up
because you meet them
on your way down.

—*Jimmy Durante*

Working hard at what doesn't work,
doesn't work.

—*Lloyd Thaxton & John Alston*, Stuff Happens

It is never too late
to be what you might
have been.

—*George Eliot*

Show me a person
who has never made
a mistake
and I'll show you somebody
who has never
achieved much.

—*Joan Collins*

If you can count your money,
you don't have a billion dollars.

—*J. Paul Getty*

Don't stay in bed—
unless you can make money in bed.

—*George Burns*

We don't know who we are
until we see what we can do.

—*Martha Grimes*

You can't build your reputation
on what you are going to do.

—*Henry Ford*

It takes twenty years
to make an
overnight success.

—*Eddie Cantor*

There is no point
at which you can say,
"Well, I am successful now.
I might as well take a nap."

—*Carrie Fisher*

Success is never final
and failure never fatal.

—*George Tilton*

I do want to be rich but I have never
wanted to do what it takes to get rich.

—*Gertrude Stein*

Either lead, follow,
or get out of the way.

—*Ted Turner*

If you hate your job, don't worry.
You won't have it long.

—*Unknown*

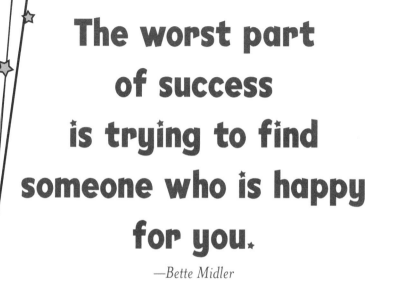

The worst part of success is trying to find someone who is happy for you.

—*Bette Midler*

Success and failure are greatly overrated. But failure gives you a whole lot more to talk about.

—*Hildegard Knef*

You are not in business to be popular.

—*Kirstie Alley*

Perseverance is failing nineteen times
and succeeding the twentieth.

—*Julie Andrews*

Don't get mad;
get everything.

—*Ivana Trump*

Knowledge is power,
if you know it about the right person.

—*Ethel Watts Mumford*

Winning

may not be everything,

but losing has little

to recommend it.

—*Dianne Feinstein*

Be bold.
If you're going
to make an error,
make a doozy.

—Billie Jean King

You can't be brave if you've only
had wonderful things happen to you.

—*Mary Tyler Moore*

I have succeeded [in my career] by
saying what everyone else is thinking.

—*Joan Rivers*

If at first you don't succeed, cheat, repeat until caught, and then lie!

—*Unknown*

Success is simply a matter of luck. Ask any failure.

—*Earl Wilson*

I have yet
to hear a man ask
for advice on how
to combine marriage
and a career.

—*Gloria Steinem*

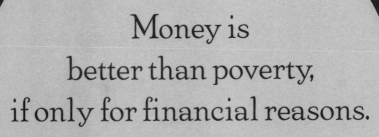

Money is
better than poverty,
if only for financial reasons.

—*Woody Allen*, The Early Essays

If at first you *do* succeed,
try not to look astonished.

—*Unknown*

Nothing defines human beings better
than their willingness to do
irrational things in the pursuit
of phenomenally unlikely payoffs.

—*Scott Adams,* The Dilbert Principle

If you always do what interests you,
at least one person is pleased.

—*Unknown*

Whenever you fall,
pick up something.

—*Oswald Theodore Avery*

It is not our abilities that show who we are— it is our choices.

—*J.K. Rowling,* Harry Potter and the Sorcerer's Stone

I have a new philosophy. I'm only going to dread one day at a time.

—Charles Schulz

Success didn't spoil me;
I've always been insufferable.

—*Fran Lebowitz*

People will believe anything
if you whisper it.

—*Unknown*

Nothing succeeds
like the appearance of success.

—*Christopher Lasch*

Do what you feel in your heart
to be right—for you'll be criticized
anyway. You'll be damned if you do
and damned if you don't.

—*Eleanor Roosevelt*

If you can keep your
head when all about you
are losing theirs,
maybe you just don't
understand the situation.

—*Unknown*

She's the kind of girl
who climbed the
ladder of success
wrong by wrong.

—Mae West

My dad always used to tell me that
if they challenge you to an after-school
fight, tell them you won't wait—
you can kick their ass right now!

—*Cameron Diaz*

Anyone seen on a bus after the age
of thirty has been a failure in life.

—*Loelia Ponsonby, Duchess of Westminster*

Learn the rules so you know how
to break them properly.

—*Unknown*

Don't confuse fame with success.
Madonna is one;
Helen Keller is the other.

—*Erma Bombeck*

Anything worth having
is worth
working hard for.

—*Unknown*

I honestly think
it is better to be a failure
at something you love
than to be a success
at something you hate.

—*George Burns*

It's not enough that I should succeed—
others should fail.

—*David Merrick*

Every man is a damn fool for
at least five minutes every day; wisdom
consists in not exceeding the limit.

—*Elbert Hubbard*

The answer to life's problems
aren't at the bottom of a beer bottle—
they're on TV.

—*Homer Simpson,* The Simpsons

If in doubt,
make it sound convincing.

—*Unknown*

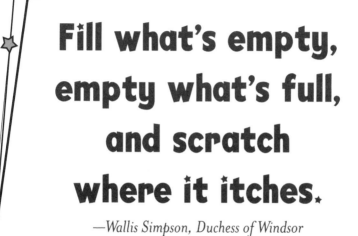

Fill what's empty, empty what's full, and scratch where it itches.

—*Wallis Simpson, Duchess of Windsor*

**Whoever said,
"It's not whether
you win or lose
that counts,"
probably lost.**

—Martina Navratilova

Take your work seriously,
but never yourself.

—*Margot Fonteyn*

If you obey all the rules,
you miss all the fun!

—*Katharine Hepburn*

Experience is the name
everyone gives to their mistakes.

—*Oscar Wilde*

If you are going to do something wrong,
at least enjoy it.

—*Leo Rosten*

Aerodynamically
the bumblebee shouldn't
be able to fly,
but the bumblebee
doesn't know that so it
goes on flying anyway.

—Mary Kay Ash

Remember,
Ginger Rogers did
everything Fred Astaire did,
but backwards
and in high heels.

—*Faith Wittlesey*

If you are riding a dead horse,
get off.

—*Variously Ascribed*

Never face facts; if you do
you'll never get up in the morning.

—*Marlo Thomas*

You get in life
what you have the courage to ask for.

—*Oprah Winfrey*

The only difference between
a good shot and a bad shot
is if it goes in or not.

—*Charles Barkley*

Behind every

successful woman...

is a substantial amount

of coffee.

—*Stephanie Piro*

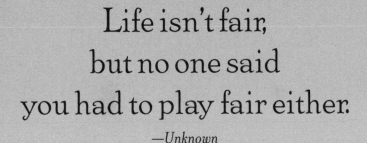

Life isn't fair,
but no one said
you had to play fair either.

—*Unknown*

Look twice before you leap.

—*Charlotte Brönte*

If you really want something,
you can figure out
how to make it happen.

—*Cher*

If you're going to put all your eggs
in one basket—watch the basket.

—*Mark Twain*

Always assume that no one
will keep it a secret.

—*Unknown*

If only we'd stop trying to be happy, we'd have a pretty good time.

—Edith Wharton

I am tough, ambitious, and know exactly what I want. If that makes me a bitch, that's okay.

—*Madonna*

I've been fortunate—
I haven't had too many auditions.
I slept with all the right people.

—Pamela Anderson

You will do foolish things,
but do them with enthusiasm.

—Colette

Listen closely to your enemies—
they will tell you your faults.

—*Unknown*

Don't believe everything you read.
I don't anymore.
I just look at the pictures.

—*Christina Aguilera*

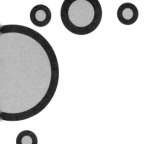

Do not do
what you would undo
if you were caught.

—*Leah Arendt*

New opportunities are often things you haven't noticed the first time around.

—*Catherine Deneuve*

There are no shortcuts
to any place worth going.

—*Beverly Sills*

Few wishes come true by themselves.

—*June Smith*

If you don't like something, change it.
If you can't change it,
change your attitude.

—*Maya Angelou*

The magic is inside you.
There ain't no crystal ball.

—*Dolly Parton*

If you think you can,
you can. And if
you think you can't,
you're probably right.

—*Mary Kay Ash*

About the Author

Amy Hatch has worked in television, journalism, and freelance writing. She is always on the lookout for the perfect quote, quip, or clever comeback. She lives in Seattle, Washington.

Contact Us with Quotes!

If you have a famous favorite quote, or personally penned pearl of wisdom that you would like to share with us for possible inclusion in a future quote collection, we would love to hear from you. You can contact us at
quotes@amyhatch.com